"Balance is a key to our sport. To have strength with that balance helps you be more effective. The harder you work in practice, the better you'll be."

OWEN NOLAN

**Sean Rossiter
& Paul Carson**

Skating
for Power & Speed

GREY*S*TONE BOOKS
Douglas & McIntyre Publishing Group
Vancouver/Toronto/New York

For John Patrick Rossiter, Pee Wee hockey player, Parkhill, Ontario.

Greystone Books
A division of Douglas & McIntyre Ltd.
2323 Quebec Street, Suite 201
Vancouver, British Columbia
Canada V5T 4S7
www.greystonebooks.com

National Library of Canada Cataloguing in Publication Data
Rossiter, Sean 1946–
    Skating for power and speed
    (Hockey the NHL way)
    ISBN 1-55054-916-2

    1. Skating—Juvenile literature. 2. Hockey—Juvenile literature.
I. Carson, Paul 1955– II. Title. III. Series.
GV847.25.R6829 2002   j796.962'2   C2002-910412-2

Editing by Lucy Kenward
Cover and text design by Peter Cocking
Instructional photographs: Stefan Schulhof/Schulhof Photography
Front cover photograph of Saku Koivu by Bruce Bennett/Bruce Bennett Studios
Printed and bound in Canada by Friesens
Printed on acid-free paper ∞

Every reasonable care has been taken to trace the ownership of copyrighted visual material. Information that will enable the publishers to rectify any reference or credit is welcome.

We gratefully acknowledge the assistance of the Canada Council for the Arts, the British Columbia Arts Council, and the Government of Canada through the Book Publishing Industry Development Program (BPIDP) for our publishing activities.

Contents

The NHL Way team

Our players

 Jaysen Mah

 Lance Quan

 Derek MacKenzie

 Keith Seabrook

 Dylan Herold

 Tara Khan

 Kellin Carson

 Luke Holowaty

 Michael Garagan

 Tory Malinoski

 Brad Irving

 Tyler Hansen

Our NHL Way coaches

Barb Aidelbaum
Hockey skating specialist (Skating Director, The Arbutus Club)

A Skate Canada triple gold medallist, Barb Aidelbaum is a nationally certified hockey and figure skating coach (NCCP Level 3). She combines a knowledge of edges, balance and counterbalancing with off-ice speed and weight training. She coaches players and teams in junior, NCAA and the NHL.

Terry Bangen
Hockey scout

Assistant coach with the Vancouver Canucks (1996–98), Terry Bangen coached two national junior teams, including the 1996 world champions. He has coached three Kamloops Blazers Memorial Cup champions—with Ken Hitchcock, Don Hay and Tom Renney—and was head coach at McGill University in 1995–96.

Ian Clark
President of the Goaltender Development Institute

Ian Clark is one of hockey's foremost goaltending coaches. He has mentored numerous goalkeepers at the NHL, minor pro, major junior and NCAA levels. Ian was a featured presenter at the 2000 International Coaches' Conference in Vancouver, B.C. He does consulting work for the Florida Panthers and Vancouver Canucks.

"Finding openings to shoot from is a mental skill. You have to be able to read the play." Getting to those openings in time takes quickness.

ZIGGY PALFFY

Foreword

Have you seen old films of Bobby Orr and Guy Lafleur skating end-to-end through entire teams, going top shelf for the winning goal? The other guys seem to be standing still. Oldtimers say they miss those days, that they sure don't make hockey players like they used to.

They're right. Even today's hockey greats seldom go end-to-end with the puck. Not even speedsters like Paul Kariya and Pavel Bure. Why not?

Because almost every player in today's National Hockey League is a good skater. Today, an NHL team's fastest skater might be a defenseman like Scott Niedermayer or Bret Hedican. Checking forwards like Todd Marchant and Brian Rolston are often faster than their high-scoring teammates. More than ever, offense is built on speed and quickness. Mike Modano and Teemu Selanne shift into overdrive crossing their opponents' blue line, jerseys billowing out behind them, but they don't leave their opponents standing still. Nobody does that in today's NHL.

Even along the boards and in the corners, skating counts. Being solid and balanced on your skates like Peter Forsberg and Bill Guerin is more important than ever.

Jeremy Roenick knows that in today's tight-checking game, the way to get space on the ice is with speed and agility. Speed forces defenders to back off or get burned. Get too close, and Joe Sakic can move sideways, get a step on you and be gone. The only cure for an opponent's speed is speed of your own. That's why *Hockey the NHL Way: Skating for Power and Speed* is so important.

There is an old saying in hockey that good teams make the puck do the work. That means passing the puck rather than lugging it up the ice. But the puck only does its work when the team is skating.

So today's NHL style is more of a team game. And no skill is as important as skating. You need agility and balance, control, quickness, speed and power—just to be in the game.

Peter Twist
Strength and conditioning coach, Vancouver Canucks

Introduction

Skating is the most important skill in hockey. It doesn't matter how hard your shot is, or how tough you are along the boards or how you can dangle the puck. If you can't skate, nothing else matters.

Improving your skating means making changes in your hockey habits and routines. Just having this book in your hand and flipping through it could be the first step toward making the most of your hockey talent.

The key to better skating is to become stronger. At any age, you can get stronger by doing simple exercises. Many exercises don't need equipment, and they can be done off the ice. But you must make time for your fitness routine.

Another important part of your fitness program is becoming more flexible. That means warming up before you work out or practice and doing stretching exercises afterward. Stretching the right way works all the muscle groups you use to play hockey.

These changes—organizing your time better, and adding more strength and flexibility—come first. But understanding how your skates work and how to use them better is the biggest single improvement you can make to your game.

Hockey the NHL Way: Skating for Power and Speed shows how the fastest and most powerful skaters in the National Hockey League use quickness, agility and speed to make their other skills more deadly. This book will show you how to add quickness with fast starts and changes of direction, and add straight-ahead speed with full stride leg extension. Most stops in hockey are pauses before you go somewhere else. We'll show you how to skate hard, stop and make your getaway in a smooth set of steps.

We provide those simple improvements. You supply the willpower and the love of the game that make everything else possible. The best thing about improving your skating is knowing you are doing everything you can to be as good as you can be—in the greatest game there is.

Hart and Norris Trophy–winner Chris Pronger's full extension and balance, seen here as he beats a checker, give him power and surprising speed for a big man.

> When I was 15 or 16,
> I worked on moving my
> feet as quick as I could.
> I think that helped.
> I always try to do that.
> It helps build both
> quickness and speed."
>
> ADAM DEADMARSH

To begin with, you need to know about four simple improvements you can make to the way you skate. Learning them is easy. Applying them to your skating style is the hard part. In the upcoming pages, we will put these four keys to use in each of the moves you make most often on the ice. They are:

First: Get into better shape. Skating the right way takes more strength.

Second: Use a lower, more balanced stance on your skates. Bend your knees and ankles more.

Third: Know where your skates are under your body, and learn how to use the edges of your skate blades.

Fourth: Fully extend your drive leg on every stride. Hip-knee-ankle-toe. Every time.

Apply these four tips to each skating skill in this book, and you will take your biggest steps forward as a hockey player.

The keys to better skating

If you want to skate right, you have to get stronger. More strength in the right places allows you to adopt a lower stance, use your skate blade edges better and get a full extension on every power stroke.

NHL teams know that. They have strength and conditioning coaches who test each player's fitness, then design off-ice workout programs to make them better athletes and hockey players.

It's the same with you. The first key to better skating is to build strength in the core of the body— the abdominal wall and the muscles that radiate out from there.

In other words, you have to work out to become a better skater. You don't need a rink to do that. Almost any space will do.

STRE

NGTH

"My speed didn't come naturally. I had to work on it. Since I was five, we did skating drills. I think it has to do with starting to skate early."

SERGEI SAMSONOV

A few simple pieces of exercise equipment can help you develop more core strength and be more solid on your skates. If your team doesn't have this equipment, visit your local gym.

Swiss ball

Many hockey players use the Swiss ball, a big plastic balloon, to help them do abdominal crunches. Use the Swiss ball to hold your legs up while you do crunches. Or lie face up on the ball, with your feet on the ground. Crunches develop the abdominal wall, which is a hockey player's strength platform.

Balance board

For regular balance training, try using a balance board, a disc or rectangular platform mounted on a pivot. Just keeping the board

Doing crunches on a Swiss ball helps Kellin build his abdominal wall.

Standing on the balance board develops Michael's balance and agility.

Brad's ball toss starts with flexed elbows and knees, then he fully extends.

Core strength

level while kneeling, sitting or standing will work your upper body, lower body and abdominal area. As your balance improves, you will be able to stay on the board longer.

Medicine ball

A medicine ball, a heavy stuffed rubber ball, can improve your upper-body and abdominal strength. Pass the medicine ball back and forth with a partner using a two-handed chest pass. Remember to bend your knees and elbows when receiving a pass.

Combinations

Use two or more pieces of equipment in the same exercise to get more from the activity. Combining different pieces of exercise equipment in new ways helps bring new life to old drills and can make them more effective. Do these off-ice exercises and you'll see direct payoffs on the ice: your muscles won't tire as quickly, you'll stand taller and straighter, bend your knees deeper and longer, and you'll have better balance and agility.

Swiss ball and medicine ball

Sit on a Swiss ball facing your partner and play catch with a medicine ball. Or sit back-to-back on Swiss balls set close together and hand the medicine ball off to one another: twist to your left to give, twist right to receive, and vice versa.

Mix and match

New twist to the old sit-up: throwing a medicine ball from the Swiss ball crunch position.

Every part of Kellin's upper body works as he tosses the ball to a partner.

Ball catch on the balance board—a new Olympic sport?

Balance board and medicine ball

Stand on a balance board and give and receive passes with a medicine ball. Squat in a deep knee bend, find a good balance with your elbows tucked into your sides and your hands out in front, ready for the pass. A partner 6 feet/2 m in front of you passes the ball at chest level. As you catch it, try to stay balanced on the board. While your upper body is dealing with the medicine ball, your abdominal wall and legs are working hard to keep you balanced.

"I did a lot of skating. Power skating, hockey and figure skating. I was on the ice a lot. In some ways it came naturally, but I had a lot of coaching."

SCOTT NIEDERMAYER

One way strength exercises pay off on the ice is better agility and balance on your skates. Controlling your movements on the ice is the first step toward adding speed and power to your skating.

Much of the game of hockey is played in small spaces. Being able to evade another player when you have the puck or stay with an opponent when checking—doing these things requires agility.

Balance means being ready to move in any direction, to take hits, to pivot or turn with the play, often while skating. Well-balanced skaters like Tony Amonte and Mats Sundin have their skates under their body mass and their upper bodies leaning forward but upright, and almost still—even as their legs are pumping at top speed.

AGILITY

& BALANCE

"Balance and agility help me skate faster. They give me time to make that first pass out of my zone. Good agility and balance also protect me from hits."

TOMAS KABERLE

Creating a solid base

Your stance makes everything else possible. If your stance is not right, your skating will not improve. To get into the right position, think of sitting in a chair:

- Bend your knees more. Seen from the side, your thighs should be almost horizontal.
- Line up your front knee at least a couple of inches ahead of the toe of your skate.
- Keep your back straight and hold your head up.

How a lower stance works

A lower stance makes you solid on your skates. It puts your body mass over your front, or glide, skate. That improves your balance.

Keith's ready position: deep knee bend, shoulders almost level, head up.

Almost like sitting, Keith's deep knee bend puts his knees ahead of his toes.

In motion: knees flexed, weight balanced, body extended, head up, arms reaching.

Stance

A deeper knee bend lets your power stroke drive farther back and to the side. And, with your body closer to the ice, you have a lower center of gravity. The lower you can get to the ice, the harder it will be for opponents to knock you off your feet.

With your back straight and your head up, you are balanced from side to side and from front to back. You are ready to see everything, go anywhere. Your first step could be in any direction.

Try this stance right now, where you are, without skates. It will feel awkward at first. Your thighs will start to hurt very soon. That pain tells you why you have to get stronger, and where.

The power stroke

Once your body is lined up over your skates, the secret to staying balanced when you are skating is keeping your feet, as much as possible, right under your body mass. It's that simple. That's how you get the most power from every stroke.

When your power stroke is done, bring your drive skate—your back skate—quickly back under you, in line with your hip joint. At that moment you are totally balanced over your glide skate—your front skate.

Return your recovering skate low to the ice. It should come almost close enough to your glide skate to touch heels. Keep your glide leg in a deep knee bend while the drive leg fully extends. Recover, and you are balanced over your skates and ready to explode with another power stroke.

Practise by touching heels with every recovery.

Body positioning

Toe, knee, head all lined up, glide knee an inch or two ahead of the toe.

As his drive skate recovers, Dylan pushes off his front inside edge.

After fully extending his drive skate, Keith shifts his weight to the glide skate.

Body positioning checklist

■ Head, hips, glide knee and skate are in a straight line up-and-down, and balanced.

■ Either way you look, front to back or side to side, the player is as balanced as possible.

■ Feet are under the body and outside the hips only on the power stroke.

"For me, there is a huge difference between speed and quickness. Quickness is more of a reaction, a quick movement to the puck or a player in the corner."

JERE LEHTINEN

We all know what it's like to be out of control on skates. It's the first feeling we had on the ice.

The key to being in control at all times is becoming aware of your skate blade edges. Every movement on the ice uses an edge to take you where you want, when you want to go.

You can skate sideways, stop and go, and do tight turns without striding—just by using your edges. You can also link those moves without stops or pauses along the way—just by using your edges.

When you're in control, you don't think, you just react. The game flows as the puck moves from player to player and team to team, and you flow with it. Less effort, more action.

C O N

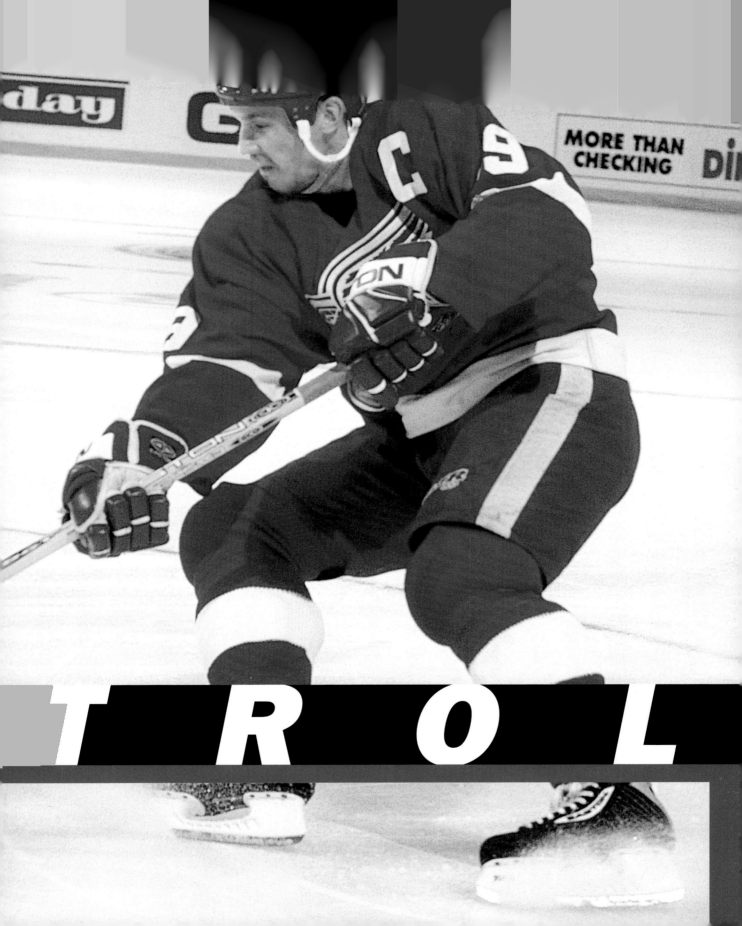

Check out your edges

There are inside and outside edges on your right and left skates. And because you skate both forward and backward, you use eight edges in total. If you are weak on one edge, you will lose control or fall.

Using your edges

As you shift your weight forward, you use the front part of the edge. Shifting your weight back puts you on the back half of your skate's edge. Leaning one way or another, or reaching out with your skate, brings an inner or outer edge into contact with the ice.

Most of the time, you use only one of those edges on each skate to stop or to change direction. If you are aware of your

Edge control

Pay attention to your inside and outside edges as you practise any skating skill.

The lower body does the work, but twisting the upper body helps.

Edge control is the key to stopping, turning and moving sideways.

edges once you are in motion, slight shifts side to side, forward or back can take you in a new direction or speed you up—all with very little effort, and without stopping or starting again.

Weighting and unweighting

Often, to make quick changes in direction or spinning moves (called pivots) you lighten the weight on your skates by slightly straightening up from a bent-knee position. The word for this is "unweight." Unweight your skates and you can pivot faster.

When to do a tight turn

The tight turn is a U-turn on ice. Done right, you can come out of a tight turn faster than you started into it. That makes it a good move for a puck-carrier trying to shake off a checker. Paul Kariya is a master of the tight turn.

It is also a good way to react when the puck changes hands. When the play changes direction or reverses, a tight turn lets you stay in the action. Now you are speeding in the other direction, uncovered, either with the puck or ready to receive it.

How to do it

Skate hard to where you want to make the turn. As you prepare to turn, step into it with your lead foot and hip, allowing your upper body to twist into the turn. Bend your knees and put your body

T I P :
The tight turn is not really a U-turn. Do it right, and you leave more of a question mark on the ice. And on the face of your checker.

Making a sharp left turn, Tara sets it up with a deep knee bend.

She points her stick to the left, helping twist her upper body...

...which brings her out of the turn with more power. Note her deep knee bend.

Tight turns

weight on the front part of your edges as you start the turn. Point your stickblade in the direction of your turn. Roll your wrists on your stick to help your upper body turn. Both feet point forward, positioning your inside skate just ahead of your outside one. Keep your weight over the middle of your skates.

Weight the back outside edge of your lead skate—the inside skate—to finish. Drive off the back inside edge of your outside skate to power away. Cross over with your outside leg to finish the turn.

"Speed doesn't come automatically. Speed definitely is inherited; there's no question. But I think you can improve it by 10 per cent if you work hard in the off-season."

BRIAN ROLSTON

When to do a crossover

After the forward stride, the next most important basic skating skill is the forward crossover. You probably already know how to do it, but here's how to do a better, faster crossover.

Done right, a crossover can help you add speed as you move to one side or the other.

The difference is more power from a lower stance, and twice the push by fully extending both legs. You are getting two pushes instead of one.

How to do it

As you skate forward, keep your knees bent deep. Weight the front outside edge of your inside skate and the front inside edge of your outside skate after you cross. Carry your stick in both hands with the blade on or near the ice in front of your body.

T I P

Try not to lean into the turn when you do crossovers. Hold your stick with both hands, close together, and keep the stick-blade on the ice.

Push hard with your inside foot as the other foot is about to step over it.

With the crossover complete, Luke is ready to push off his inside edge.

Pushing off the front outside edge of your crossover foot adds power and speed.

Crossovers

Push to the side hard and under on the front outside edge of your inside skate, as you transfer your weight and cross your outside skate over your inside one. Keep your crossover skate low.

Use the front inside edge of your crossover foot to bite into the ice as you shift your weight over that foot. Push back and to the side as you fully extend your leg.

As your skate reaches its fullest extension, step to the inside with your inside foot.

When to do a crossunder

This move is actually much simpler than the forward crossover. It only seems difficult when you're not yet comfortable skating backward.

As a defender, you can use a crossunder to add speed while checking an opposing puck-carrier, usually in the defensive zone. And as you are skating backward, you can also control the gap between you and the puck-carrier, and move sideways faster. Even if you're not a defenseman, remember that when your team doesn't have the puck, each skater is a defender.

How to do it

Skating backward with your knees bent, your outside foot rarely leaves the ice. It forms C-cuts to add power to each step. Keep your weight over that outside foot.

Crossunders

Fully extend your crossunder foot to add more power to your stride.

Tara shows good leg reach, pulling from the front inside edge of her inside foot . . .

. . . and finishing her stride by fully extending the leg that crosses under her body.

To begin, step with your inside leg out wide, reaching as far as possible. Grip the ice with the front inside edge of your inside skate and pull that skate under your body. Shift from the inside edge to the front outside edge of that same skate and drive hard, fully extending your leg. Reach inward again with the inside skate, grip the ice, and repeat.

Most players find doing crossunders easier one way than the other. Work on doing them both ways.

"Some players have a lot of speed but don't know when to use it. Use acceleration, on and off, and stop. Use sprints, here and there. It makes opponents worry more."

TEEMU SELANNE

Why pivot?

In the flow of a game the puck changes hands hundreds of times. You switch from offense to defense and back again several times each shift. Some athletes play only offensive or defensive roles for long periods of time. Hockey players have to do both, and make the change in a heartbeat. Sometimes that change means going from forward to backward skating, and back again, in split-seconds. The fastest way to make these changes is to pivot from one to the other.

Forward-to-backward pivot

This pivot is also called the "Mohawk turn." You can use it when your team loses the puck and you are caught behind the play. Skate hard into your team's zone then pivot from forward to backward skating, staying between your check and the goal.

Pivots

Skate hard, glide, then turn on the front inside edge of your lead skate.

Luke has transferred weight to his opposite skate . . .

. . . now he moves backward, weight balanced, doing a C-cut with his left skate.

How to do it

Start by skating hard, then deepen your knee bend and glide on one skate.

Shift your weight over your glide skate and begin opening your hip on the side you want to turn to. Turn your knee and your skate in the direction you want to go. Turn your head and shoulder that way, too.

With your heels together and your toes out, turn on the front inside edge of your glide skate. Shift your weight from your glide skate to the one pointing backward.

Backward-to-forward pivot

This pivot is a key skill for defensemen. Often defensemen or backchecking forwards skate backward to face a rush coming into their zone. If an opponent dumps the puck into a corner, the closest defender should pivot quickly to go after the puck. Always look over your shoulder to keep an eye on other players and figure out where you can play the puck once you get to it.

How to do it

Shift your weight on to one skate and glide backward on that foot. Turn your head and shoulders in the direction you want to turn.

Skating backward, weight on his front inside edges, Kellin leans forward . . .

. . . turns his head and upper body, opens his left leg, points that skate, pivots . . .

. . . and bends his leading knee, fully extending his drive leg afterward.

Pivots

Open your hip on that side. Turn that knee and skate outward so that your skates are heel to heel. Shifting your weight over your glide skate, and maintaining balance and edge control, is key.

With your glide skate, complete a full stride driving in the direction of the turn. When you transfer to the forward edge, your weight is over the middle and back part of your skate. As you shift your weight forward, drive forward hard off your back skate.

Most passing, checking and battling for the puck takes place within small areas of the ice. Winning these mini-battles is more important than sheer end-to-end speed. The first step is all-important. Moving in the right direction with that first step is the key.

Think about how most goals are scored. Few are scored off the rush. More often, a series of defensive mistakes leads to a score. Most goals come off turnovers.

To take advantage of those mistakes, you need to read the play, anticipate the action and react to the sudden change of possession. If you are near a loose puck, you have to move fast to get control of it. If you are away from the puck, go to the nearest open space. Remember . . . the first quick step is key.

QUIC

For two-time 50-goal scorer Peter Bondra, his speed means getting to the puck sooner, with a step on the defender, and having time to look at the goalie.

When to stop

Often the first thing to do when the puck changes hands is to stop on a dime. Stopping can be the quickest way to change directions because you don't even have to come to a full stop. A one-foot stop and crossover can get you moving in the new direction faster than a quick turn.

A quick stop is also a way to shake a checker and protect the puck. Cross the offensive blue line at top speed and, if your way to the net is blocked, stop dead in your tracks. Make sure your checker hasn't stopped, too. Then look for a pass receiver in the middle. If your teammates are covered, or you can see no pass, get the puck deep into the zone along the boards.

> **T I P**
> Always skate hard to a loose puck, even when you feel no pressure. The sooner you get to the puck, the more time you have to make the right play when it's on your stick.

Hands on stick for balance, Keith stops on the outside edge of his inside skate.

Looking in the direction he wants to go, he crosses over with the other skate . . .

. . . and gets going with short, choppy strides on his front inside edges.

Stops and starts

One-foot stop and half turn

With both hands on your stick for balance, turn to one side, lean back, flex your knees and drive the front outside edge of your inside—or trailing—skate into the ice.

Look back in the direction you came from. Your front skate will be off the ice as you stop. Cross it over the skate you stopped with and drive hard off the skate that's still on the ice. Let go of your stick with your lower hand.

Start taking choppy steps with the front inside edge of your crossover skate, driving your arms forward to add power to your strides.

Hockey stop

This is a two-footed stop. Use it when you have no choice but to come to a halt.

It's a good idea to have your stickblade on the ice when doing the hockey stop. It makes a third point of contact with the ice. Most players stop better one way than the other. Often it will seem easier when you're turned to the side you shoot from. Work on stopping both ways.

How to do it

As you turn sideways to stop, the heel of one skate should be level with the toe of the other. Your trailing skate should be slightly ahead. Hold your stick in both hands, and learn to keep your stickblade close to the ice when you stop.

Hockey stop

Turned sideways, Jaysen comes into the stop with his knees almost straight.

He digs his edges into the ice and bends his knees to add more stopping power.

He sees the pass—his stop allowed him to shake his check.

TIP
Don't be afraid to fall when you are working on stops and starts. The ice is slippery. Everybody falls. The trick is in how fast you get up again.

Relax your knee bend going into the stop. That helps unweight your skates.

Now drive the front inside edge of your front skate and the front outside edge of your back skate into the ice. Flex your knees, using them as shock absorbers to get more force and stopping power, as your edges cut into the ice.

Don't just stop. Stop, and read and react.

If you're stopping to lose your check and you are open, have your stickblade on the ice. Look for the pass.

"It is who you're playing against that makes you improve your skating. In Europe everybody knows how to skate. To excel over there, you better be faster than they are."

BRIAN RAFALSKI

Get going

There's no point in stopping just to stand around and watch the game. You want to get going again right away.

Always try to convert your straight-ahead energy into a turn, so you can go in another direction. If you can't do that, sometimes you need to set out from a standing start.

V-start

Use the V-start to get going from a standing position when you need a fast, explosive burst of energy.

How to do it

Balance your weight on the front inside edges of your skates—heels close together, toes out. Your knees are about shoulder-width apart, deeply flexed and bent outward.

Explosive starts

Skates forming a V, stick in one hand, Derek drives off his front inside edge.

Up to five choppy strides later, he starts to fully extend his strides.

By the time he makes the blue line, Derek shows good drive-skate recovery.

T I P

Try not to rush around all the time. Keep a little bit in the tank so you can explode into a higher gear when you see the right opening.

Explode from this V-stance with three to five choppy strides, staying on the front inside edges of your skates. Take small, quick, choppy steps.

Lead with your chest. Keep your head up. Hold your stick with your top hand, driving your arms front to back to add power to your straight-ahead speed.

After three to five short steps, start to extend your strides. Then begin fully extending the drive leg to build speed.

Crossover starts

This move gets you going sideways. Use it after a two-foot stop, with one crossover step leading to a V-start.

You can do a crossover start while skating either backward or forward. It is used most often by defensemen to block the way of a puck-carrier.

But it can be a great move to get around a defenseman when you have the puck. Joe Sakic can look like a freight train coming in on a defenseman, then move just as fast to the side, getting himself open to take a shot.

How to do it

From a stop, turn your head and shoulders in the direction you want to go. Keep your head up and your shoulders level. It can also help to point your stick where you're going.

T I P

When you master the crossover start, learn to do it without looking where you are going. It can be a puck-carrier's secret weapon.

In the ready position you are balanced on the outside edge of your inside blade.

Turning his upper body shifts Brad's weight to his inside leg.

His outside leg crosses over. He drives off the left front outside edge to gain speed.

Crossover starts

Cross over with your outside leg, keeping your crossover knee low for good balance. You want to just clear your stationary skate.

After you cross over, reach sideways in the direction you want to go with the skate on that side. Grip the ice with the front inside edge, and pull inwards. After the first crossover step, twist your body into the V-start position for two or three more short quick strides. Keep your head up and on a swivel. A sudden sideways move can put you in traffic.

Goaltenders are the most important players on the ice. Nowhere else is reading and reacting and moving quickly more important than in the net. For a goalie, footwork, edge control and agility are vital. As a goaltender, you can play your position using a mix of styles. But, whatever style works for you, there are some skills all goalies must master.

Positioning

You can't stop the puck if you are not in position. Positioning is made up of three parts:

- Your angle, which means being on the line from the puck to the middle of the net.
- Your depth in the net along that line.
- Your balanced stance.

Goalie footwork

Tory is standing up on the shot line. He can reach any shot that is on the net.

A C-cut with the inside front edge of his right skate starts him back into the net.

After backing in to the post, Tory starts across the goalmouth with a T-push.

Each is important, but none more than angle. Even if you've got a great glove hand, it's no good to you if you can't reach the puck.

Once you are on that shot line, move in or out, depending on where the shooter is. For point shots, be at the edge of the crease. As the shooter comes closer, be ready to back in to cover the deke.

Even butterfly goalies spend most of the time on their feet. Stand on your inside front edges and balance your stance: front to back with a deep knee bend so your stickblade is flat on the ice, and side to side with your feet wider than your shoulders.

"Movement and footwork are the keys to positioning. Practise moving post to post, out along the shot line and back into the net every time you step on the ice."

ROBERTO LUONGO

Future Hall-of-Famer Patrick Roy starts a sweep check across his net after the puck-carrier behind the net reverses direction. It's a race to the far post.

But what if the puck is moving from side to side?

You have to move with it. There are four ways to get across the goalmouth: two "up" moves and two "down" moves. The most common up moves are the T-push and the shuffle. Use an up move when the play is still outside the faceoff dots. The closer the shooter or the pass across the crease, the faster you must get across. That's the time for a down move.

The T-push

The easiest way to cross the goal is with a T-push. Point outward with the toe of the foot on the side you want to move to. Push off the front inside edge of the other skate. Shift your weight to the glide skate. Keep your knees flexed. That helps you hold your normal stance, gives you better extension and helps keep your stick on the ice. Plus, it makes it easier to stop exactly where you want to. Learn to go from post to post with one push.

T I P :
Once the puck-carrier commits to the deke and you put your pad down on the side he or she goes to, give a little kick ahead with that foot. That makes it harder to lift the puck over your pad. And it often directs the rebound away.

Tory T-pushes to his stick side. Lead leg turned out, pointed where he's going.

The shuffle. Tory takes big steps, but keeps his stance while moving sideways.

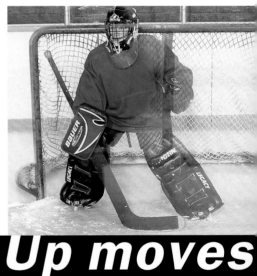

He keeps his stick on the ice all the time. One more step takes him to the post.

Up moves

The shuffle

With the puck closer, shuffle across. The shuffle keeps you in your shot-blocking stance all the way across. Keeping your toes pointing straight ahead, take a small step sideways with the foot on the side you want to move to. Then close your legs by bringing the back foot under you. Repeat as many times as you have to. Keep your knees flexed. Stay square to the puck.

When the puck crosses near the crease, you need to slide from post to post quickly. There are two ways to do it in one move—stacking the pads and the butterfly slide. When you get there, most of the goalmouth is covered down low.

Stacking the pads

Stacking the pads is one way to defend against a pass from one side of the net to a receiver on the open side. You want that receiver to see a wall of goal pads. This is a big-save move.

How to do it

Start with a T-push in the direction you want to move, pushing off hard with the inside front edge of your back skate. Flex both knees, so your back leg pad is down on the ice as your upper body leans back. Bend your lead leg, then extend it across the

Down moves

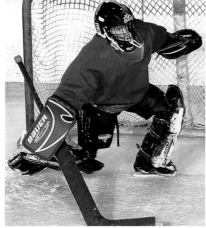

Tory begins with a T-push, fully extending his trailing leg.

Knees flexed, the trailing pad is now sweeping under his body.

He stacks his pads, adds his glove for height and keeps his stick ready for a return pass.

goalmouth. When your trailing knee and hip hit the ice, sweep that back leg along the ice to a position under the lead pad.

As you finish, your pads should be staggered. Keep the top pad ahead of the bottom one to block a quick-rising shot or deflection.

Complete the move by placing your upper arm along the top pad to make the stack a little higher. If it's your glove hand, you are ready to catch a shot or deflection going higher than your stack. If it's your blocker hand, you've got another 75 square inches/480 sq. cm of the wide part of your stick to work with. Reach out your low arm square to your body along the ice to control a return pass or rebound.

Butterfly slide

Not all young goalies can do the butterfly slide. It takes strength and flexibility. And, the bigger you are, the more effective this move is. But, if you can do it, the butterfly slide is a way to get across the goalmouth in one move. You can keep your eyes on the puck more easily than when you stack the pads.

How to do it

As with the T-push, your back foot points ahead of your body. Reach with the leg on the side you want to move to, and push off

T I P

Keep your chest high doing the butterfly slide. You are going down, opening up the upper part of the net. Keeping your chest up helps cover that opening up high.

Push off hard from the post, keeping the lead pad square to the shooter.

Tory's pads are almost flat on the ice, covering everything but the five-hole . . .

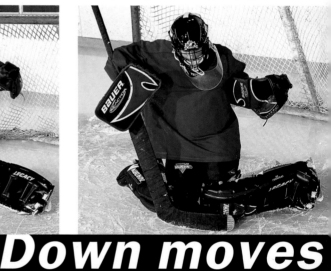
. . . which he shuts with his trailing pad. He keeps compact. His body is upright.

Down moves

hard with the inside front edge of your back foot. Get your lead pad down fast and slide to the opposite post. Now bring the trailing pad quickly to the ice and close the five-hole with it.

The trick is to keep yourself compact. Keep your arms tightly at your sides, and close that five-hole fast when you get to the other side. Finish with your stick covering what's left of the five-hole. Or set it paddle-down to cover more of the ice.

Power is energy in motion. In hockey that means movement. And skating is one of the fastest ways a human can move.

In skating, you get power from your stride leg, which adds to both speed and balance. You need power to fight your way along the boards or keep your place in front of the net. You have to keep your legs moving when sticks and bodies are holding you up.

That takes strength. It takes strength to keep a deep stance and get the most out of your skating stride and extension. But it is worth the effort. When strength and proper skating form come together, one result is more speed. And the need for speed is greatest in the fastest game on two feet.

POWER

& SPEED

"When I first started skating, we skated without a stick. Later, we skated with a stick, but not the puck. Become a good skater before doing anything else."

MARIAN HOSSA

How balance leads to power

Power is hard to see, but it's like a coiled spring that releases energy as it unwinds. If you can control how much energy you release in what directions, you will be a controlled, powerful skater.

One reason great skaters like Mario Lemieux and Teemu Selanne make it look so easy is that their upper bodies hardly move at all—even when they are skating at top speed. When you're balanced over your skates, you can focus all of your energy in one direction—straight ahead—without losing any to sideways wobbles.

The secret is to have your body weight balanced over your skates as much of the time as possible. Your body has to be centered over your glide skate when you recover from your

TIP
By keeping your head still even as you skate at top speed, you can see around you better. Your head swivels easier when it is still.

At the moment of stride recovery, Lance has both feet under him.

Lance starts into a good low recovery. His head is lined up over his glide skate.

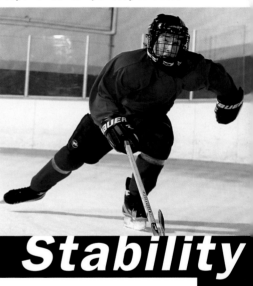

Even with full extension, Kellin's upper body and head are perfectly balanced.

Stability

power stroke. This shift in weight over your glide skate prepares that leg for the next power stroke. That puts the mass of your body behind the power stroke. After each full extension of the drive leg, recover as low to the ice as you can to get your other leg's power stroke off to a quicker start.

Power checklist
- Keep your head up, your eyes forward and your upper body still.
- Drive your arms straight ahead to propel yourself forward.
- Keep your body mass over your edges for better balance.

Hip-knee-ankle-toe

Some of the fastest players in the NHL, like Scott Niedermayer, seem to glide around the ice, hardly working at all. Once your stance is balanced, the key to more speed is your power stroke. Think of each big joint—hip-knee-ankle-toe—as adding more power to your stroke.

How to do it

Your power stroke should be out to the side and back. It has to be outward for you to get the most out of your front inside edge. It has to be behind you to push your glide skate forward.

Feel it happen. Your power stroke should start at the hip, driving your biggest leg muscles out and back. Next, you

Full extension

Both feet are under Luke's body. His drive foot is ready to uncoil.

That final toe flick gives one last shot of power. Head, knee, foot, all lined up.

Seen from the front, Luke's extension causes a slight weight shift to that side.

TIP

"When you get to your top speed, stride out as far as you can. Let your body relax. Nice and slow and long strides."

TONY AMONTE

straighten your knee. Then you extend your foot at the ankle. A final toe flick completes the stroke.

It takes more time to do all those things right. That's what makes skating the right way look easier. Your power stroke is slower, your legs are pumping less, but you are skating faster.

Listen to your skates on the ice when you get full extension. They sound different. There's a raspy *snick!* at the end of the stroke. It's that toe flick biting into the ice.

That's the way to make the most of your strength. You need to convert all the strength you have to speed.

"It took me years to realize that hockey is played with the lower body. My off-seasons are geared toward leg strength. I increase my quickness through plyometrics."

KEITH PRIMEAU

Off-ice training

The base for adding more speed and power to your game is more strength. More strength for hockey comes from dry-land training. In the off-season, you train to improve. During the hockey season, doing these exercises helps you maintain your fitness.

Plyometrics

Jeremy Roenick does plyometrics. So do Simon Gagne and Ed Jovanovski. Plyometrics are jumping, hopping and bounding exercises that are good for on-ice quickness and agility. Young players can benefit from plyometric exercises too. But be careful. Plyometrics are high-risk exercises, so proper instruction is essential. Always try for a soft, stable landing and a quick reversal of direction.

Building strength

Tara moves quickly in the opposite direction and "pops" her feet off the floor.

Bring your knees to your chest to clear the bench. Take off and land with knees bent.

Make sure the box is solid. Don't jump any more than 18 inches/45 cm.

Bounding exercises

Big, long, bounding strides work the muscles in your legs when you push off and when you land. You can bound forward or sideways, from the floor, a bench or a wooden horse.
- Stand on the balls of your feet with your knees bent.
- Push off, driving your arms forward to give you height. Bring your knees to your chest.
- Land on your entire foot when touching down sideways.

Good for: stride length and power.

Deep squat jumps

Squat jumps develop leg strength.
- Squat on the back of your feet with your knees deeply bent.
- Push off the balls of your feet by shifting your weight forward.
- Land lightly on your feet, bending your knees in one fluid motion.

Good for: low stance.

Squat running and lunges

Squat running develops your quadricep muscles (front of the thigh).
- Squat on the balls of your feet with your knees deeply bent. Place your hands behind your back, with one hand holding your opposite wrist.
- Run around the room, staying balanced in the squat position.

Good for: low stance.

Lateral bounding: Start with a deep knee bend and do another between hurdles.

Front foot moves first, toward falling bean bag. That's how Kellin snags the bag.

Shuffle laterally to each pylon, do a deep knee bend to touch it, and repeat.

Exercises

Lateral running

Running from side to side imitates your skating drive stroke.
- Place 12 markers in two lines about 10 feet/3 m apart. Alternate the markers so that they make a zigzag pattern.
- Run to the first marker. As you turn to run to the next marker, plant your outside foot. Bend your knee deeply and push off to the next marker.
- Repeat with the remaining 11 markers.

Good for: stride length and power.

Always warm up before you do any kind of exercise, but especially before playing hockey. If your team does warm-ups together, great. If not, do them on your own. Jogging is a good warm-up exercise.

Take some extra time to stretch at home after you return from the rink. That's the most comfortable place to stretch. Do it at your own pace and choose exercises that work for you. Make it as enjoyable as possible, and stretching will become a lifetime habit. Add other exercises as you begin to see the benefits.

And you will see benefits. Stretching prevents injuries. It makes you more flexible. It will help you skate better. Take the time after every game or practice. It's a workout in itself.

STRE

Knee bends: Stand with your arms at your sides, feet flat on the floor. Bend your knees. Hold for 45 seconds. *Good for:* calves.

Calf stretch: Stand facing the wall, one toe against the baseboard, the other foot 3 feet/1 m behind facing forward. Lean your head and raised elbows against the wall. Switch legs. Hold for 45 seconds each leg. *Good for:* hamstrings (back of thigh), calves.

Forward lunge: Kneel on one knee, keeping your front leg ahead of your body. Extend your back leg as far behind you as it will go. Place your hands on the floor in line with your front foot to support you. Press down from the groin. Switch sides. Hold for 45 seconds each leg. *Good for:* hamstrings.

Quad stretch: Sit with one leg bent to the side. Touch your opposite foot to the bent leg's knee, using your arms behind your body

Calves & hamstrings

Quad stretch. Lean gently back and forth to stretch your quadriceps and lower back.

Hamstring flexor. Reach for your ankle or your flexed foot, pulling back for more calf stretch.

for support. Lean back to stretch one leg, then forward to stretch the other. Switch legs. Hold for 45 seconds each leg. *Good for:* quadriceps (front of the thigh), hips, lower back.

Hamstring flexor: Sit with one leg extended in front of you. Touch your opposite foot to the inner thigh of your extended leg. Lean forward, keeping your back straight. Switch sides. Hold for 45 seconds each leg. *Good for:* hamstrings, hips, lower back.

Triceps stretch: Stand with one arm behind your head, touching the top of your opposite shoulder blade. Hold the elbow of that arm with your opposite hand. Gently press down on your elbow, pushing your hand down your back. Switch arms. Hold for 10 seconds each arm. *Good for:* triceps, rotator cuffs (shoulder).

Arm twist: Stand with one arm behind your head, the other bent low behind your back. Start by touching the finger tips of each hand; work at grasping your knuckles. Switch arms. Hold for 5 seconds each arm. *Good for:* triceps, rotator cuffs.

Triceps flexor: Drop down on your hands and knees. Stretch one arm straight ahead of you on the floor. Grasp the elbow of your straight arm with your opposite hand. Lay your head on your bent arm. Press down on your elbow. Switch arms. Hold for 10 seconds each arm. *Good for:* triceps (back of the upper arm).

Triceps stretch. Press back with your head to add to the stretch.

Triceps flexor. Hold for 10 seconds each arm. Also good for your lower back muscles.

Hip flexor. Opening your hips will improve your upper-leg turnout for pivots.

Shoulders & neck

Forearm extension: Drop down on your hands and knees. Turn your wrists so that your fingers point back toward your body. Lean back. Hold for 20 seconds. *Good for:* inner wrists.

Neck stretch: Lie on your back with your legs in front of you, knees up and bent. Grasp your hands behind your head. Lift your head straight up. Hold for 5 seconds. Work up to sets of three. *Good for:* neck, upper back.

Hip flexor: Sit with one leg extended in front of you. Bend your other leg toward you, holding the ankle in one hand and the foot in the other. Pull your foot toward your body until you feel a gentle stretch in the muscle. Don't force the stretch. Switch legs. Hold for 30 seconds each leg. *Good for:* groin, hips.

Groin flexor: Sit with your legs spread as wide as you can. Lean forward, keeping your back as straight as possible. Work toward touching the floor in front of you with your chest. Hold for 30 seconds. *Good for:* groin, hamstrings, lower back.

Groin stretch: Sit with your legs in front of you, knees bent and the soles of your feet touching. Hold your toes to keep your feet together. Lean forward, keeping your back as straight as possible. Hold for 45 seconds. *Good for:* groin (especially good for goalies).

Back and hips

Groin flexor. Keep your back straight as you lean forward, toward the floor.

Groin stretch. Hold your soles together, pressing them to your body.

Torso twists. Try to get your crossover knee to the opposite-side floor.

Torso twists: Lie on your back with your legs in front of you, knees up and bent. Cross one leg over the other at the knee. Grasp your hands behind your head. Keeping both shoulders on the floor, touch your crossover knee to the floor on the opposite side. Switch sides. Hold for 45 seconds each leg. *Good for:* gluts (bum), lower back.

A point-a-game player, Vincent Damphousse is also a great checker. Here he pressures the puck-carrier, then stops with his stick in the passing lane.

Special thanks

First and foremost, special thanks to the parents of our NHL Way players. Thanks also to Arthur Pincus and (as always) Denise Gomez of the NHL, to the NHL players who shared their secrets and the NHL team public relations people who forwarded them to us.

Thanks to the Vancouver School Board for use of the University Hill Elementary school gym. We are grateful to Twist Conditioning Inc. for use of their gym equipment. And to Pat Logan and the staff of the University of B.C. Thunderbird Winter Sports Centre for making us feel welcome at the Father Bauer rink. To the Titchener & Associates Chiropractic Clinic, thanks for the stretching program. Thanks once again to Mike Cox of Cyclone Taylor Sports, official NHL Way outfitters.

Finally, thanks to Will Harvey, an original NHL Way player, for his inspiration and support of the new players.

Credits

Photography

Photography by Stefan Schulhof/Schulhof Photography, except as indicated below:

Photos by Bruce Bennett Studios:
Front cover, pp. 7, 18, 21, 23, 33: Bruce Bennett
p. ii: Brian Winkler
pp. 4, 15, 41, 51, 55: Jim McIsaac
p. 8: Wen Roberts
p. 11: Peter MacCallum
p. 12: Len Redkoles
pp. 26, 42: Dale MacMillan
p. 29: James Baker
p. 37: Andy Marlin
p. 38: Christopher Pasatieri
p. 59: John Russell

Photo of Peter Twist courtesy the Vancouver Canucks
Photo on p. 17 by Jessica Bushey/Vancouver Canucks

Photos on pp. 34, 47 by Mitchell Layton